A BOOK OF FOLLIES

A BOOK OF FOLLIES

KATHRYN DASZKIEWICZ

Printed by imprintdigital
Upton Pyne, Exeter
www.digital.imprint.co.uk

Typesetting and cover design by narrator
www.narrator.me.uk
info@narrator.me.uk
033 022 300 39

Published by Shoestring Press
19 Devonshire Avenue, Beeston, Nottingham, NG9 1BS
(0115) 925 1827
www.shoestringpress.co.uk

First published 2017
© Copyright: Kathryn Daszkiewicz
© Cover image, How to Take a Great Selfie, by Marshal Arts

The moral right of the author has been asserted.

ISBN 978-1-910323-89-2

ACKNOWLEDGEMENTS

Acknowledgements are due to the editors of the following publications and websites where some of these poems first appeared: *The Dock*, *The Frogmore Papers*, *The Interpreter's House*, *New Walk* and *Orbis*.

Running Before the Wind: Poems About the Sea edited by Joy Howard (Grey Hen Press)

Something Happens, Sometimes Here: Contemporary Lincolnshire Poets edited by Rory Waterman (Five Leaves Publications)

Into the Wilderness won first prize in The Bramley Apple Competition (2013) and was published in Southwell *Folio Magazine*.

In memory of Sarah Chisholm Rodgers (1904–2000)

CONTENTS

THE LOADED GUN

Around the Reeperbahn near where we stay
graffiti blooms. You say that you dislike
those crude cartoons that fire cold concrete
and breed or bleed on brick or plasterboard.
But one piece makes you laugh. You capture it –
on a wall exposed by houses ripped apart:
a girl with a gun (tied to a selfie stick)
aimed at her head. She's smiling stupidly
making a futile peace sign. Brief, bright art
that draws the eye to what's no longer loved
speaks to the hurts it seems that I invite
by letting you back in. I tell a friend
I trust that I have lapsed. And he is blunt:
going there with you is equal to self-harm.

HOTEL VIEW: SEPTEMBER '14

Carnage. A No Man's Land
of condemned offices. It's dusk.
In silence, the long reach
excavators brood.

A wall of innards
gapes where the building's
been unseamed. And as
stray wires score an aching
sunset,

       he wraps his guilt
around him like a shield.
His guilt that floors
her every second night
they ever snatch. Arms

by her side, she'll never
make the move. Now,

after nine, machines
grind into action
and pound the open
honeycomb of rooms.

Something implodes.
Sunday she is a broken thing.

And grit is bitter in
her stopped mouth.

SOAR

The sky is right, for once, we have an hour
alone. You're going to teach me how to fly
so you give me the lines and take the sail
and stride across the patch of green we've found
devoid of picnickers and football games.
You throw what should be dancing into air –
it drifts for seconds then it crashes down
again. Again. Back to the wind, I steer,
determined I should win the upper hand
this once I hold the strings, though I don't feel
I do. I try too hard. Apparently,
I over compensate. So I relax
and let the breeze dictate then lean away.
I think I have a lot to learn from kites.

SEEING THROUGH

You told me you were going
somewhere in France. I wasn't
sure where. Dragged me round
town for the bits and pieces
that you hadn't borrowed:
ski socks, thermal gloves.

I thought I'd hope there'd be
a card. But lately it's been
too cold in the sun. And when
I try to picture you it's as
a figure on a downhill slope:
all white on white. I cannot

make you out.

YOU HAVE THE WHEEL

as we up and wind through shadow
crossed green lanes going
back on ourselves again and
again although we know the

right way.
    The light shifts
in your head
                your reason turns

to being friends *for good*
this time you say. As if

we can uncross this Rubicon,

still be ourselves. You run
a bath to sluice away
those old near futures.

Come down all fresh.
Announce you've left

the water for me.

It would be skin
on skin
at one
remove.

I won't be
lying
in it.

SKIN

It's closeness that's the key – being at one
with someone who, just like her, isn't at home
in his own skin; who feels a knife slide over
inadequate wrists in the houses of great men;
to whom a preponderance of blue plaques
is a slap in the face; who has a goad
as a reflex saying *You've never. You may never*
… and time's a bitch.

　　　　　　　　We can't slough our skins
dramatically like snakes – we are reduced to dust
speck by ignominious speck. But to rejuvenate
a snake finds something harsh to rub against.
What of that night of doubt when, fit to burst,
she wove barefoot through damp grass to the tent
to find he'd zipped their sleeping bags together?

FRIENDSHIP MATERIAL

is serviceable stuff that's made to last
in greys and homely reds – those weaves that keep
the wind out. Not silks shot through with hues
which only hold their promise in the light
like sun projecting stained glass on the flags
of afternoon cathedrals where the golds
fragment as patterns in kaleidoscopes
a dance of broken halos in the dust;
like frail Murano glass fired to seduce
millefiore and aventurine:
a thousand blooms caught up in threads of gold
which lead into the dark and lose their gloss
unwinding and unwinding. And undone.
There lies the worm – far cry from the homespun.

SO

By the box hedge near the gallery
I'm stranded on a bench. Book in my hand
sun on my back. I've lost the thread.

I know that you will come
but not from where. I should

have taken cover, taken coffee
beneath a parasol in the garden café.

Stirred by a breeze
the plane trees wreathe
elusive Morris patterns on the flags

then suddenly you loom across the page
and take the words
from under me.

ON HOW I FEEL ABOUT A CERTAIN PERSON

There's something about
the way you stand
that is the sum of you:
all six feet two –
head slightly bowed
and shoulders (to a close
observer) taut as if
the elastic that is
your confidence
and runs
from your toes to the top
of your spine
(where it's attached)
was cut just short.

WHAT LIES

A peeling wooden board
warns PRIVATE but you swear
that once you walked to Gonerby
that way. I think the path you mean
is further on. There's a signpost but it points
to where grass grows waist high. No obvious
route through. So, do we dare?

I'm up for forging our own way:
skirt north along the A1 then branch
off across the scrub. Or enter
the wood close to this awkward verge
we're teetering on – where spruce and cypress
keep green counsel that we might have
shared. But you are crossing to the other side
which has a pavement. And I follow.

We climb a stile, but as you're scared of cows,
we edge around a field where summer
shows her heels in hedges
heavy with the hung heads
of elderberries. Out of the sun
brambles lift green fists.

We wind up in a village I don't much like:
the ivied old somehow not quaint enough
while new build's angular and brash
despite no end of climbers – roses
passion flowers. But the church on the hill
affords a valley view: a sweep of slanting fields –
the future on a good day.

We carry on past ostentatious drives
and chessboard gardens. You see
someone you know. Regret
not waving.

Soon (beyond the hill) we'll join
a lane that leads to a grove of old sweet chestnuts.
But as the slope begins you slow and turn –
are wanting to go back.

IN THE DARK

I've never seen so many molehills as this afternoon, as we drive
in silence, ice stubborn in shady places. I wonder what entices
a mole to rear out of its close tunnel, poke its small pink snout
into biting air. There are mounds along the roadside verges;
sprawling brown settlements by garden walls; oneupmanship
colonies in the choicer villages, where old stone meets new glass.

I imagine moles with their awesome foreclaws
made for going forward, tiny eyes repelling dirt
as they forge their way in darkness. I'd rather see a mole,
confirm what's there, than have a show-house lawn. So I'm alert
for a small black form emerging,

to gauge the temperature, wait for the earth to settle.

If I stand still, make no vibrations, maybe a mole
will heave into the open from that place
where tunnel leads to tunnel. But all I see

are two buzzards circling the tower
of the church we've come to view.

Neither you nor the ground
makes any move.

A SOLITARY WOMAN ON THE VERGE OF NIGHT

Sunsets grow
in abandon through these
winter months as if
whoever weaves
the warp and weft of sky
finds once deft fingers numb.

Roguish strands of light
pursue their own ends
lose themselves in hues
that never ought to mix.

A drift of cloud
or darkness screens
their shame.

HOW THE END BEGAN

And afterwards her own house
felt strange. She slid the bolt

back, stepped outside. The trees
were not themselves. It was so cold

it didn't thaw all day. Everything
in rime and nothing making sense

a world on hold. And footprints
that led back to what was home

and those he'd made
into beyond

subsumed in sheet ice.

LEARNING TO LOVE THE COLD

In the afternoons of these bitter days
there is something to be learned
from the ache of old glass
the way it yearns
for frost flowers
lost to sunlight.

DESIRE LINES

Desire lines are the paths that pedestrians make when they deviate from an official path.

(i)

Duck under the wooden fence and lie
eye level with the trefoil, yellow
as the bypassed warning sign
dizzy and pink as cliff edge thrift.

As a lazy aeroplane unzips the sky
each bloom's an echo of a coarser
folklore name: cow rattle,
cockle, cuckoo's stocking.

Let skylarks tittle-tattle on
their fine trapeze
while pressed grass rights itself
and the foamy wake dissolves.

(ii)

Tracing the path her heart has scored
in her own hand

she pictures a seasoned palmist's
shock at the dares and deeps of it

how, staring at the floor, she'd hint
where it would lead only to giddy heels,

straining to see
the line that represents the head

faint
as conscience

no hope of toeing it

(iii)

We thought we were the only ones
who dared to snake down through the mahonia
shunning the safe way with its metal handrails
shin deep in thorny shrubs. But when
a muddy trail materialized
and the council hacked away the tangled bed
to cover it with acrid smelling bark
the ground was strewn with cans,
crisp packets, garish wrappers:
the telling detritus of subterfuge.

CLOSE CALLS

When only the past is green
she'll remember the waterfalls.

Not English trickles
but those impossible plunges –
places she thought

she'd never go. Secretive
ferns; spurious mists –
where
afterwards

even at a distance
you cannot see for spray –
too fired to notice

deep trees ringing
with the cries
of hidden birds.

RAPTOR

A creature so other
must be watched

like the tiercel
all the breeding season

a swift dark anchor
circling the spire.

Kee-ark. Pigeons tumble.
Kee-ark. He calls. All day

he calls and echoes
in the dark. Marks

out his prey from way up high
and way back when. She might

have turned before that stark
collision in mid air

that ripped the breath away
as beak met viscera.

And left a limp thing,
all the lights torn out

METEMPSYCHOSIS

There is a tradition amongst seamen that the souls
   of old sailors after death, occupy the bodies of albatrosses…
– E. H. Shackleton

On the day the cat licked its fur
against the grain
they knew a storm would come.
The ship's bell clanged
with no man near.
Its slack rope swung
like a noose.

Offguard, he'd put his left foot
forward on the planks
that Friday they'd set sail,
when land had shrunk
to a speck in his eye
was gone.

His corpse

sewn into sailcloth
was weighed down
with stones. It sank and sank.

His soul,

in shape much like the caul
he wasn't born with,
slipped through the seams.

Unfurling in the murk
it slowly surfaced;
rolled round in foam
it passed from wave to wave.

Feathers

of spray caressed it.
The cold was a strange embrace
and when high winds made the sea surge
it was flexing spindrift wings.

They spread and spread
and the next squall launched it skyward

soaring, soaring.

ELEGY

Cymbals clashed like waves
while the fluid vibes of a guitar
floated the big white bird
across our screens each Thursday
for at least a month that winter.

Its two chord ambience
was haunting.

But no one could have guessed
as it spun from a million record players
or unspooled from reel to reel
stretching its wings across a rolling sea

that the current
was already turning
treacherous with hooks
and it was ghosting its way
to the depths.

THE VISION OF HIROSHI HASEGAWA

Shoji Yamamoto rubs his eyes. But when
he opens them, the birds are there still:
ten ghostly shapes on Torishima's slopes
as if they've risen from the ash.
As if they've been reborn
out of the fires the feather hunters lit
to smoke them from their nests.

Even when their plumage set alight
or when the wooden clubs rained down
on the heads of these scorned *gooneybirds*
they wouldn't leave their eggs. They clacked
their bills in anger. The island heard.
It shuddered at those tons
of bloodied snow shipped out
(for pillows, mattresses and ladies' hats)
and buried at least a hundred harvesters,
under lava as they slept.

And what was once a village is a tomb
upon a birdless waste.

When he hears the news of their return,
after a time another man will come.
He'll build up terraces
to stop the dust from sliding;
channel the mudslides from the clumsy chicks.
He'll build a dam to stem the sometime floods
and plant miscanthus grass to bind the ash.

He'll clamber across basalt, then he'll climb
the island's barren ridge. From grey sand
he'll gather sun-bleached bones,
place them with reverence on a smooth, flat stone.
He'll burn incense there. And then he'll pour

seawater for the restless spirits to drink. Set out
squid and flying fish. He'll wait in silence
meditate a while. Then read a sutra.

His words will drift
across the grave of Tamaoki village
down to the cliff below
where a small colony
of short-tailed albatross
have graced the land again.

KINGFISHER ON THE WITHAM

Three sullen steps
ahead you saw him first.

And though you deigned
to give a branch by branch

account of where he hid
I couldn't get my eye in

till he moved, low willow
to low willow. Later I

thought even you
could never dim

the flare of him
that swift, bright nib

rewriting patterns
in my winter head.

He flew, his breast
the colour of desire

but perching, turned
and ice extinguished fire.

WALKING THE LINES

On the fast train, each hamlet,
each town's a blur.
Another year that couldn't
fruit. There might have been
room at the inn
but we never stopped
arriving in body at an end before
the mind caught up to grasp
all that we could
have seen, have been.

But where the ghosts
of branch lines lie buried,
wholly beneath the green
we wander between
banks leafing into vaulted holloways,
go with the flow of rivers
made of grass. And when our hands
snag on the scrolling briars
we taste the blood
and it wells up again.

BRINK

We tune into the sounds
on the cusp of dusk and real dark.
This is a liminal world
where the river on the fringe
of town remembers wildness.
On the far bank spikes of gunnera
stand Gothic in the gloom.

When I look up all I can see
is space between the canopies of trees.
But the gadgets in our hands
translate their cries
so we know bats are about.

A flit. A cinder. Slivers of old night
in a gnat-to-gnat dance
are common pipistrelles.

We alter frequency
and their soprano cousins add their notes
to this moonless opera. While over water
as we lean on the balustrade of the white bridge
Daubenton's – the water bats – whirligig
whiz to catch mayflies
in the busy chase.

I'm in a place
of otherworldly calls
where root meets water
beast is bird
drawn like a shaman
to slip through a crack
in the bark of an old oak
as the light returns.

ALL HALLOWS DAY

The mist was palpable as if
it seeped in from the other side
last night. But mid-morning

sun had made it through,
fired up a host of dragonflies
riding each other by the full canal

as if the world was dying. Though fog
had scuppered other flights
and moorhens kept to the fringes

in the shade of past-their-best bulrushes
and the towpath's half-stripped hedges
were bloodied with hawthorn,

they flew by, fizzing, dizzy, fused together
light as our breath and bound
for blue elsewhere.

NEST

Taking the sunlight now they perch and preen
their pinks and greys on a bare loop of briar.
Weave in their beaks, all day they've come

and gone. I sneak to peer up through the barberry –
prickly, dense – a dark criss-cross of branches
and I sense why they are drawn to thorns
to evergreen. To know it's there

behind that screen snug in the centre
thicket deep unseen, cobwebs to bind moss,
lichens and wisps of softer stuff

lined with a thousand feathers.
That's enough.

AT THE HEART OF THINGS

The tree stands by the footpath
on the way to town. It's bare now.
So you can see an empty nest is couched
in a deep V where two main boughs
have gone their separate ways.

The tail end of a hurricane
that surged down from the north
couldn't dislodge it – even though
it stripped the slates from nail-sick
roofs nearby. Tore the last stubborn
leaves from the beech hedge, toppled bins.

Was it made by two? Or did
a single pair of wings fetch twigs and roots
and grass and moss and mud?

Then in the spring,
did birds take turns to warm the eggs
or was it one at the tree's heart
that played a waiting game?

Bowed down by shopping
she's trailing behind couples
heading home.

Watching them,
she feels the knot inside her chest
(where something fluttered
once – almost airborne),
pull tight again.

CHARM

All summer wresting dandelions
out of the earth before they launch pale stars
I'm in the company of finches

weaving their song
above the traffic's urban drone
threading their golds though magnolia

whose flowers, pointing skyward,
pray to the breeze
to spare them day on day.

It's only when the winter's well
iced in, I find the nest they hid
safe in a crook. As if it was made

proof by that same spell that will,
in spring, ignite the bush
to flame.

GREAT CRESTED GREBES

They bob like courtesans
too sleek for northern waters,

elaborate coiffures
unspoiled by the breeze,

each one a maiko
an apprentice geisha

child of the dance
and from another realm

called kanyukai
a flower and willow world.

PRAIRIE AFFAIR

Something is missing – what, I mustn't say;
unwritten rules evolve. I'm forced to lie
in this bed, prairie wide. And I am prey.

Read me between the (small hour) sheets. By day
smooth out the fact we've tangled. And deny
something is missing. What? I mustn't say?

I'll text the view from my hotel. Today
I'll wander by the Tyne alone. Get by.
The bed is prairie wide. And I am prey

found wanting yet again. So you hold sway:
a wolf alert for a chance alibi.
Something is missing. What, I cannot say.

Deliver me or take me. Either way
there will be grief, my little world awry.
This bed is prairie wide and I am prey.

A temperate grassland's not for us. We play
a dangerous game. I doubt you will reply.
Something is missing – what, I mustn't say.
This bed is prairie wide. I'm willing prey.

CLOSURE

He was inclined to mine for darker stuff –
which took the shine off each time we struck gold
or what I took for it. Enough wasn't enough:
daylight brought gilt to me; guilt made him cold.
I surfaced to a wan and struggling sun –
a fading coal behind grey bars of cloud:
over a heap of slag, ton upon ton
of overburden. The whole landscape cowed.
Deep down a tiny yellow bird revived
its feathers dulled and pale from years of dark
but in its wing, its eye, a spark survived
and burned to try the air and, like a lark
above, in years to come, to spy unseen
that mound of dust and ash begin to green.

WAKE

Now you can see. That simple
rowing boat has been there
all along. Make for a kinder
sun. There was never an after
in that cold harbour
where oil coloured the shallows
with its treacherous rainbows.

And your wake will fan into
a glorious V: a white tail
full of eyes; a thousand bubbles
in a champagne dance.

While in the room
where you were laid
sheets will be pulled
over an absence
and shutters
magnify
the keening
of the wind.

SHE LONGS FOR SEA FRET

and those nights wrapped
in the small room five fields from the coast
when you could see no further than the laburnum
or the wall with the sometime gate.

Those nights with the foghorn sounding though gauze
and the muted chant of a train escaping south
and parents just beyond the hardboard wall,
white bubbles of anaglypta that her fingers
still recall – bubbles that never burst.

And while those cold coves beneath the cliffs
are laying themselves open in the darkness,
to sea spray and an audience of stars
she lies curled into herself like the cowrie,
white and smooth, picked from the sand at Marsden
before that surge of waves which split the rock arch.

And what if the cotoneaster under the bay
window reaches up and up until it's holding
the thorned stems of the pink rose that has spurned
the trellis? And the ivy, not satisfied with smothering
the red brick wall by the kitchen, slithers across
the flat roof of the porch. If mermaid and maygold
follow their lead and creep across the tiles
to meet the plaited creepers from the west
shedding their petals in a heap which in a fairy-tale
would be spun into the stuff of dreams?

The one she can recall, the one that came back
night after night, played out in the space between
the houses, behind the double gates.

There was a stranger generating sparks – and fire
threatening as they swirled and struck.
She saw the stars orange against the sky – Orion's belt
tightening round her throat, the only constellation
that she knew. The unknown Plough was somewhere
over the grainy sea which frothed and raged
spewing its waves against the Cat and Dog Steps
(where hundreds went to soak up weekend sun)
sucking the waters from the undertow
of the shelf beside Trow Rocks.

But the black bolts hold fast. She longs for sea fret and –

THIS DISTANCE

(i) Here Again.

We climb dunes bound
with ribbed and shining grass
which spreads both root and shoot
to stop the sands from shifting.

A small boy struggles to control
a kite his father's launched for him.
It flails and falls.

And when you note that children are oblivious how
the memory of such days, spent in a moment, here,
beside the sea, will shape what they become

I know you're thinking of that boy you were
before that sweeping tide which no amount
of marram grass could stem.

You flip the glass egg timer in your mind
replay the past until the grains run out.

(ii) Seagulls in the Dust

You draw seagulls
flying in the dust
on chests-of-drawers
in land-locked B & Bs.
Deft, curling Vs
and though they cannot soar
their wings extend
to albatross proportions
and weigh you down.
Their silent cries are
raucous in the dark.

(iii) Making it Better

He's wheeling with the gulls
across another coast
where rain means lemonade
or fish'n'chips.

And afterwards
always a rainbow
arcing through clouds
to mend the sky —

a plaster
holding what is split
together.

(iv) The Seashore Pocket Guide

tells me that *holdfast*
is a root of sorts
keeping a seaweed
anchored to the rocks.

It grips
but cannot nourish.

(v) Wreck

In a north westerly gale
she dragged her anchor
and the sands took her
as she ran ashore.

At low tide
festooned with bladderwrack
barnacles and dulse
she shows herself.

You know she's always there.

Get them to play at pirates all day long
one tourist website says.

But tides are treacherous here
and the beach criss-crossed
with deep cut channels
where
undertow
can knock you sideways.

Even from this distance.

(vi) Mostly You Hold Back

They spend their lives
in vertical burrows
under sand

but today the strandline's
strewn with razor shells
at angles

hinting *catastrophe*
in hieroglyphs
no one can unlock.

(vii) Made to Float

In your six year old mind
it was life or death –
the touch and go drama

of do or die hopscotch
as, barefoot, you leapt
between foes
on the strandline.
Right in your element.

Today there aren't many.
Those that dot the beach
have lost their luminescence
although each jelly dome
has a faint amethyst tinge
the fading filament of a blown bulb.

And heading back
your footsteps flounder
in the uneven sand.

(viii) The Lack

of a windbreak
is what you remember

that two-poled flag
vivid with deckchair stripes
staking a claim: this patch
of sand is ours. Until
the tide
turns.

Families have tents now –
those magic pop-up kinds.
Fluorescent.

Easy to
lose your bearings on a beach where
reference points can
shift: a distant

yacht; some
picnickers; a
kite.

    You scour
the shrinking sand
for what you left.

In the rank confetti
tangled in the wrackline:
an empty mermaid's purse.

(ix) Memorial

Placed where the beach begins
(or where it ends)

faded silk roses
loll beside a stone

near where the waves effaced
those eager footprints.

He'll wander always
through blue summers

toward a sea
inside your restless head.

THE SECRET LIFE OF HOUSES

Maybe a house doesn't shed its memories,
walls absorbing shreds from conversations
which reach a certain pitch.
Plaster might, when silence acquiesces,
like a shell held to a willing ear,
unloose its powdery secrets, voice on faint echoing voice
repeating what was said this hour
a year or many more ago.

Maybe the shiny surfaces in rooms
store moments of intensity –
freeze frames. If you stand
in a place when the light's right
on anniversaries, they'll ghost across the gloss paint,
white on white. And sometimes images
will overlay each other.

Maybe floorboards hold the agitation
of those who cross them
but of bare feet only. Should you trace
the looping grain with a receptive palm
you get a sense of footfalls
from the past – but nothing more.

It may be just the passing cries of birds
or shadowy games played by the sun or moon.

Or a shift when the chimney exhales phantom smoke,
the hearth at the heart of the house
remembering flame.

BEHIND HIGH WALLS
GWENLLIAN AT SEMPRINGHAM

(i) Moons

It's whispered Gilbert's mother, growing round,
dreamed that the full moon slid down from the sky
and settled in her lap. It was, she said, a sign

the child in her belly would wax great. He did.
His painted halo's luminous as the moon
that gapes across these fens on a clear night.

My own months are not measured by the moon.
That flood is stopped. Another gift
unused. My mother died in giving light to me.

My family is dispersed across this land –
caged princes, chastened sisters – all to stanch
the blood that might be spilt should we be free.

So I gaze at the moon I am allowed – an English moon
over these endless fens. Here it will never snag
on the jagged crowns of hills.

(ii) Captive

I ate an oyster once. Unlocked it
from its shell. There was no pearl

inside its grey and slippery heart
no moon on a grey night caught

between the clouds. I have read
the gospel of St Matthew where he tells

about a pearl so special
a merchant sold

his everything to own it.
I see my story in an oyster shell:

pearl of great price
that never saw the light.

(iii) Sunset on the Fens

is stained glass freed
from lead. The colours

kiss and marry, bleed
into new unions –

pink as the limbs of cherubim
or gold as angel halos.

Sometimes the clouds
are edged with silver

like the drawn sword
of a warrior saint. And

when the year is old
copper and flaming orange

vie to set the sky alight.
This is not hell; but something

in my bones tells me
never to call it home.

(iv) Clouds

Carmel, Sinai, Gaash, Gareb,
Ephraim, Gilead, Hermon, Seir.
These are names I give the clouds –
but only when I deem them grand enough.

Mountains I've never seen. I'd like to think
that on the journey eastward I was soothed
by the sing-song undulations of the hills,

rocked by a wordless lullaby
that rose and fell until earth
lost its joy to the judder
of hoof on stark, flat ground.

There's none to tell me tales
(the kind that merge with memory)
about my infant self. But I know
that Wales boasts hills – and mountains too.
And I miss them – somewhere they are in my blood.
I do not know their names.

(v) Monument

The ripple of a wimple
is quite plain
side-on in upright stone
fresh-hewn
from Penmaenmawr
unchiselled.

The head's bowed
like a nun
at prayer,
asking perhaps

that she might,
in her lifetime, know
the rise and fall of hills,
of her own tongue.

As she once did,
it stares across the fens
a land oppressed by skies
sometimes so leaden
she could not bear the weight.

ON THE FIRST MORNING OF NOVEMBER

The last of the three was the colour of smoke
its back, before it saw me, already arched,

not in the customary stance of feline warning
but as if shape-shifting: as if

its spine were about to stretch
and propel it upright; tail tauten

to a broomstick. But I had caught it,
a dirty Cinderella stop-out, whose hour

was slipping fast and the dark hump
of its backbone – that bridge to the other side –

would be impassable in daylight
and leave it crouching at the crossroads.

THE NINE LIVES OF MY LOVER

He's quite oblivious to the fact
that in my mind, he is a cat.

How many lives he's lost
through feline indifference:

the careless scratch, his night
on night desertion. How is it he

keeps coming back from the dead
end alleys he leads me down

looking for another place to sink
his claws? He has one end in mind;

but since the eighth small death
he's failed to sense that something is amiss.

Now that the number nine has come around
I will not resurrect him with a kiss.

WHAT FOLLOWS

It wasn't my idea, but I went along with it
cow parsley jostling along the verge, windblown heads
leaning across the towpath to toy with our wheels

while prim stalks still upright by the hedge
rustled lace in starchy disapproval.

Cycling over asphalt was a breeze and we flew
with the ease of the swallows we saw swooping over thatch

but then we hit grass, arduous grass
for leg-aching mile after mile where the sudden blush
of a bullfinch was subsumed by briars, their pale blooms
reluctant to be coaxed into a chill June where sun was fitful.

The sudden joy of tarmac was short-lived
smoothness reverting to scrub after less than a mile

where the canal was landing strip for the clash and glide
of a swan. A cross wind played the dissonant strings
of the reeds to the warbler's strident call, while up ahead
flanked by blown bulrushes – as drizzle began for the
        umpteenth time –
a defunct lock crumbled all green with fern.

There was nothing, now to hold the waters back.

INTO THE WILDERNESS

What is a Ha-ha? I asked.
The very fact I remember it was you
who knew, shows that even then

wildness was rising, an end
to artifice in sight. Somewhere
beyond the folly, a veil

was lifting as tier
by tier the formal garden
fell away to bracken greener

than my vows. After that prim
avenue, those permitted
vistas, it was easy to follow

as the blackthorn
shed its lace
by the rise and fall

of a slattern stream
sluicing her course
through chequered shade.

TOWN BOUND

The pub had changed hands –
its usual fireside dogs a damp-furred
absence. We soon left – wound uphill through the half-wood
in the dark. Snake-shallow roots of birches tried to snare us,
no night bird sang or hooted though the leaves
(I stopped to listen) and midsummer scents
were muted by the dust stirred from the earth
where I wrong-footed trying to catch you up.

In that ginnel cramped by the fences of either-side semis
skulked the memory of a New Year's morning fox –
she was there then not there even though no gap
seemed large enough to swallow her lithe form.

The still air trapped the smoke of dying fire-pits
as we traipsed over gravel at whose edge
tall nettles, feverfew and vetch
did their suburban best
to make it green.

We crossed the main road onto a wide way
which once had been the downs
to follow the slope – all house
on 'thirties house, the same design,
and most with car-ports on their ghosted gardens.

Then on the opposite side,
a huge dog fox
pulsed rhythmically
along the middle pavement
his energy mesmeric.

Your stark urbane revulsion
made me wild.

GOING BACK

(for John)

I head inland as the sun sinks
shells in my pocket
the sea in my veins

a stone worn smooth
striped with calcite

still winding on some shore
through skeins of bladderwrack

the day's imprint slow to fade
as flutings of night tides
in sand.

On the windowsill
of my cold house
there will be no jug of buddleia
bright berries and crocosmia

no brown dog to patter
after my shadow

her salt paws padding
through my landlocked
dreams as I swim deeper

into a sleep inspired by salt air
and all the history we share
of that far-reaching coast.

BY THE WAYSIDE

Spuggy's Arch led off Moor Lane, its entrance
vaulted with twisted, wizened hawthorn
where locals tipped grass cuttings in the ditch
so it always smelt of green.

Once you'd passed the paddock where the horses
hung about, it was wild until you reached the allotments
and the path met the railway line

they warned me never to cross if I was by myself. I rarely
strayed that far, stopping at the copse which promised
owls at roost, as yellowhammers chinked and chirred
in the elder.

This drew me more than Sunday school and *Tell Me
the Stories of Jesus* though I liked the word 'yonder'.

The verse mentioned sparrows on a tree there
which somehow made it not so bad about
the empty seat left of the piano, God's sixpence
still in my pocket and the pull where my frock had caught
on the wooden stile.

They said it was bad luck to pick the May
although the hedges were thick with it
like aisles decked for a bride. The scent
was heavy. I wasn't sure I liked it
but it stirred me.

By autumn red haws blooded the bare thorns
and when you bit the sour fruit in half
a star with five points showed
beneath the flesh.

THE BEGINNING OF STARS

We called the cut (that led to Woodlands Road
from Moor Lane between the Wimpey houses)

The Ponderosa after a ranch-style 60s bungalow
that squatted part way down – the name, displayed

on a piece of oval bark, fixed to a gatepost. It was
accessed by that ancient right of way, so the path

that led to their grand entrance was wider
than the rest and slick with tarmac. Was I

impressed? By the name or its American brazenness?
The rows of sporty cars ranged on the drive?

It was probably one of those that hit the starling
I found lying there one August morning. Thug

of the bird table which hung round in gangs.
A pushy bird I thought that I disliked.

I stared as the sun brought out
those gleaming rainbows hidden in its blacks.

And in the constellations
of its breast each tiny star caught light.

CROSSROADS

Because of the accidents
they staggered the crossroads
at Moor Lane

shunted the east-west
junction sideways. Stemmed
the flow. You had to

turn right, then sharp left
to reach the coast. And crashes
multiplied – as if some resident spirit

was perturbed. That motorcyclist
slumped by the kerb of the out
of kilter route bled in my head for years.

And if you stand on that grass triangle
laid to fill the space – you feel its pull
more potent than the fields to either side.

And up ahead the sea
becomes the sky.

IN BLUEBELL WOOD

The water wasn't deep and no-one drowned
although we often slipped. But one day it was

gone. Filled in. No more green dares
on slithery boulders, dipping a sodden plimsol
into weed. No more frog spawn for our sixpenny nets.

The wood lost what I didn't know had been
the formal pond of an old landscaped garden

beyond the ruined folly where we hid
below its arches as the darkness pooled

(those don'ts that plagued us to the privet hedges
framing the houses where we were secure,
lost echoes in our ears.)

Maybe the chestnut trees, there all along
their mirrored leaves trailing in the wake of golden carp,
rejoiced in the return to wildness

summers waist-high in keck,
with dusty nettles lurking in the hollows.

A *deja vu* of bluebells late in spring.

CYPRESS IN WINTER

Even a thaw
can't reach the heart of them
or storm lash them bare
as they hug feathery branches
breathe in the blue-green scent of themselves
nurse their darks
as the year turns.

In evergreen sleep
too dense for light to probe
they loom against the skyline
chess pieces of forgotten giants
and, secure in their otherness,
blot out the spent
coin of the moon.

THE BOOK OF FOLLIES

tells me that whims made brick,
or castles in the air of actual stone
are not ridiculous to the minds that dream them.

That lone arch on the hill –
which doesn't lead to a grand avenue
with tall oaks sweeping you along
a graceful drive towards a place to rest –
is only a hollow promise
where you step from
scrub to scrub.

A gateway to perhaps,
guarded by standing stones,
the land on all sides
spiked with blazing gorse,
seems too remote
to reach.

But those faux ruins
in the grounds of stately halls
whose upkeep is a nightmare to the trusts
that take them on… Cracks
in the crumbling curtain walls
that were there from the start.
Deliberate ivy. No roof
to stop the rain.

Or stop the stars.
The romance of a Gothic staircase
spiralling up to nothing
but a fall. You know
this place and climb
to watch the clouds
part on a cuckoo land.